# Wallace&Gromit ™

# CHEESE LOVER'S YEARBOOK

Wallace's private yearbook. If lost
please do return to 62, West
Wallaby Street. Cheese reward
guaranteed!

Don't forget it's
my diary too.  G.
Reward negotiable.

# PERSONAL DETAILS

**NAME** _Wallace_ and Gromit. G.

**ADDRESS** 62, West Wallaby Street,

**TELEPHONE NUMBER** See piece of paper behind clock on mantelpiece

**DATE AND PLACE OF BIRTH**

## CERTIFICATE OF BIRTH

When and where born: Hospital 7 August

Names: Wallace

Sex: Boy

Name of father: Dad

Name and maiden surname of mother: Mum

Profession of father: Father Christmas at the Co-Op (part-time)

Signature of registrar: _A Hartnal_

## QUALIFICATIONS

CSE woodwork, domestic science, nuclear physics

I must not fall asleep in Geography
I must not fall asleep in Geography
I must not fall asleep in ... Gromit

I've got numerous Open University degrees. G.

**OCCUPATION** Technological research scientist.

Other Sidelines

Man who puts holes in Crackers
at Coltrane's Crackers Ltd.

School crossing patrolman.
Part-time window cleaner.

**VEHICLE REGISTRATION NO.** WAL 1

Favourite cheese: Wensleydale

**IN CASE OF EMERGENCY PLEASE INFORM:**

**G.P.** Doctor

**ADDRESS** The High Street

**KNOWN ALLERGIES** He comes out in a nasty rash whenever
the man from number 36 is in the surgery.

Supermarket trolleys, decimal
currency, skateboarders.

# USEFUL NAMES AND ADDRESSES

The Cheese Board
Grate Cheddar Street
London W2

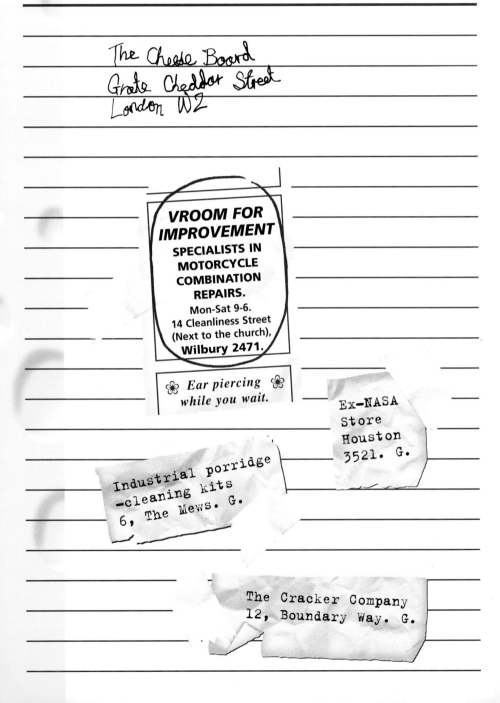

**VROOM FOR IMPROVEMENT**
SPECIALISTS IN
MOTORCYCLE
COMBINATION
REPAIRS.
Mon-Sat 9-6.
14 Cleanliness Street
(Next to the church),
**Wilbury 2471.**

❀ *Ear piercing* ❀
*while you wait.*

Ex-NASA
Store
Houston
3521. G.

Industrial porridge
-cleaning kits
6, The Mews. G.

The Cracker Company
12, Boundary Way. G.

Wallace and Gromit's Wash'N'Go Window
Cleaning Service

See what I can get
for old cooker

Sid's Scrap Metal Emporium
123 Gasworks Lane

## CRAFTY CHEESE CO.

(SUPPLIERS OF FINE CHEESES TO THE NATION)

❧

**WAPITI ROAD INDUSTRIAL ESTATE,
NETHER BARROWBY.**

Ring Mr Ratchett in Skimming and
suggest relaxing game of
dominoes sometime.

Wendolene's Wools
The High Street

5616

# YEAR PLANNER

| | January | | | | | | February | | | | | | March | | | | | |
|---|---|---|---|---|---|---|---|---|---|---|---|---|---|---|---|---|---|---|
| Sat. | - | 6 | 13 | 20 | 27 | - | - | 3 | 10 | 17 | 24 | - | - | 2 | 9 | 16 | 23 | 30 |
| Sun. | - | 7 | 14 | 21 | 28 | - | - | 4 | 11 | 18 | 25 | - | - | 3 | 10 | 17 | 24 | 31 |
| Mon. | 1 | 8 | 15 | 22 | 29 | - | - | 5 | (12) | 19 | 26 | - | - | 4 | 11 | 18 | 25 | - |
| Tues. | 2 | 9 | 16 | 23 | 30 | - | - | 6 | 13 | 20 | 27 | - | - | 5 | 12 | 19 | 26 | - |
| Wed. | 3 | 10 | 17 | 24 | 31 | - | - | 7 | 14 | 21 | 28 | - | - | 6 | 13 | 20 | 27 | - |
| Thur. | 4 | 11 | 18 | 25 | - | - | 1 | 8 | 15 | 22 | 29 | - | - | 7 | 14 | 21 | 28 | - |
| Fri. | 5 | 12 | 19 | 26 | - | - | 2 | 9 | 16 | 23 | - | - | 1 | 8 | 15 | 22 | 29 | - |

| | April | | | | | | May | | | | | | June | | | | | |
|---|---|---|---|---|---|---|---|---|---|---|---|---|---|---|---|---|---|---|
| Sat. | - | 6 | 13 | 20 | 27 | - | - | 4 | 11 | 18 | 25 | - | 1 | 8 | 15 | 22 | 29 | - |
| Sun. | - | 7 | 14 | 21 | 28 | - | - | 5 | 12 | 19 | 26 | - | 2 | 9 | 16 | 23 | 30 | - |
| Mon. | 1 | 8 | 15 | 22 | 29 | - | - | 6 | 13 | 20 | 27 | - | 3 | 10 | 17 | 24 | - | - |
| Tues. | 2 | 9 | 16 | 23 | 30 | - | - | 7 | 14 | 21 | 28 | - | 4 | 11 | 18 | 25 | - | - |
| Wed. | 3 | 10 | 17 | 24 | - | - | 1 | 8 | 15 | 22 | 29 | - | 5 | 12 | 19 | 26 | - | - |
| Thur. | 4 | 11 | 18 | 25 | - | - | 2 | 9 | 16 | 23 | 30 | - | 6 | 13 | 20 | 27 | - | - |
| Fri. | 5 | 12 | 19 | 26 | - | - | 3 | 10 | 17 | 24 | 31 | - | 7 | 14 | 21 | 28 | - | - |

| | July | | | | | | August | | | | | | September | | | | | |
|---|---|---|---|---|---|---|---|---|---|---|---|---|---|---|---|---|---|---|
| Sat. | - | 6 | 13 | 20 | 27 | - | - | 3 | 10 | 17 | 24 | 31 | - | 7 | 14 | 21 | 28 | - |
| Sun. | - | 7 | 14 | 21 | 28 | - | - | 4 | 11 | 18 | 25 | - | 1 | 8 | 15 | 22 | 29 | - |
| Mon. | 1 | 8 | 15 | 22 | 29 | - | - | 5 | 12 | 19 | 26 | - | 2 | 9 | 16 | 23 | 30 | - |
| Tues. | 2 | 9 | 16 | 23 | 30 | - | - | 6 | 13 | 20 | 27 | - | 3 | 10 | 17 | 24 | - | - |
| Wed. | 3 | 10 | 17 | 24 | 31 | - | - | (7) | 14 | 21 | 28 | - | 4 | 11 | 18 | 25 | - | - |
| Thur. | 4 | 11 | 18 | 25 | - | - | 1 | 8 | 15 | 22 | 29 | - | 5 | 12 | 19 | 26 | - | - |
| Fri. | 5 | 12 | 19 | 26 | - | - | 2 | 9 | 16 | 23 | 30 | - | 6 | 13 | 20 | 27 | - | - |

| | October | | | | | | November | | | | | | December | | | | | |
|---|---|---|---|---|---|---|---|---|---|---|---|---|---|---|---|---|---|---|
| Sat. | - | 5 | 12 | 19 | 26 | - | - | 2 | 9 | 16 | 23 | 30 | - | 7 | 14 | 21 | (28) | - |
| Sun. | - | 6 | 13 | 20 | 27 | - | - | 3 | 10 | 17 | 24 | - | 1 | 8 | 15 | 22 | 29 | - |
| Mon. | - | 7 | 14 | 21 | 28 | - | - | 4 | 11 | 18 | 25 | - | 2 | 9 | 16 | 23 | 30 | - |
| Tues. | 1 | 8 | 15 | 22 | 29 | - | - | 5 | 12 | 19 | 26 | - | 3 | 10 | 17 | 24 | 31 | - |
| Wed. | 2 | 9 | 16 | 23 | 30 | - | - | 6 | 13 | 20 | 27 | - | 4 | 11 | 18 | 25 | - | - |
| Thur. | 3 | 10 | 17 | 24 | 31 | - | - | 7 | 14 | 21 | 28 | - | 5 | 12 | 19 | 26 | - | - |
| Fri. | 4 | 11 | 18 | 25 | - | - | 1 | 8 | 15 | 22 | 29 | - | 6 | 13 | 20 | 27 | - | - |

# BIRTHDAY CHART

**NAME** GROMIT          **DATE** 12th FEBRUARY

**PRESENT IDEAS** De luxe knitting needles

Electronics for Dogs: The Movie

Roget's Thesaurus

Techno-trousers? ← ring NASA

Collar and lead

**NAME** WALLACE          **DATE** 7th AUGUST

**PRESENT IDEAS** Complete spanner and wrench kit

Novelty braces

Electric filofax

Gourmet cheese hamper

**NAME** WENDOLENE          **DATE** 28th DECEMBER

**PRESENT IDEAS** - Book token?

- socks???

- handkerchiefs??

He's got a
lot to
learn about
women. G.

# NOTABLE DATES IN THE CHEESE CALENDAR

**12 January**  St Ivel's Day, the patron saint of cheese spread

**13 February**  Shrove Cheeseday

**19 March**  World Gouda Tossing Championships, The Hague

*crown*

**7 April**  Parmesan Sunday

**11 April**  Mouldy Thursday

**13 May**  Cheese Bank Holiday (Papua New Guinea)

**22 June**  Miss Cheddar Gorgeous competition

**30 June**  Trooping the Stilton

**4 July**  British Cheese Lover Society AGM (all mice excluded)

**31 July**  Dutch expedition plans ascent of EC cheese mountain

**9 August**  Anniversary of invention of mousetrap

**17 August**  Start of National Safety Council's 'Eat Caerphilly' campaign

**28 August**  Brie Day (France)

**1 October**  International Olympic Committee meet to discuss possible inclusion of Gouda tossing for year 2000

**3 November**  National Cracker Day

**1 December**  Decorate the Christmas Cheese

# PERSONAL DIARY DATES

13th March  New shipment of Camembert arriving

12th February

My birthday. G.

7th August  Mine

**Sheffield**
**Wensleydale**

Home Match - 26th October

ADMITS 1

MAN AND DOG ANNIVERSARIES

1 year Diamond      6 years Pearl
2 years Emerald     7 years Silver
3 years Gold        8 years China
4 years Sapphire    9 years Crystal
5 years Ruby        10 years Bone

# YEARLY ACCOUNTS  JANUARY-JUNE

## FOR WALLACE AND GROMIT ENTERPRISES

### Debit

| | |
|---|---|
| Pack of assorted nuts and bolts | £2.49 |
| Subscription to 'Jams of the World' magazine (binder and issue two free) | £46.00 |
| Motorcycle combination repairs | £51.00 |
| Year's supply of continental crackers (special offer!) | £39.00 |
| Bills (electric, gas, phone, water, newspapers, food, cheese) | £396.28 |
| Gromit's birthday present | 95p |

### Credit

So much for man's best friend. G.

| | |
|---|---|
| Mrs Warburton's gardening | £2.50 |

# JULY–DECEMBER

## Debit

| | |
|---|---|
| Compensation to Mrs Warburton for destroying plants | £38.95 |
| More bills | £445.00 |
| Home rocket-building kit | £26.50 |
| Shelves for Mrs Warburton (goodwill gesture) | £15.00 |
| Hydraulic jack to free Mrs Warburton from beneath collapsed shelves | £95.00 |
| Flowers to Mrs Warburton in hospital | £2.25 |
| Annual subscription to Cheese Society | £12.00 |
| Lawyer's fees (Mrs Warburton case) | £10,000.00 |
| Lawyer's sandwiches (smoked salmon and prawns) | £6.60 |
| Lawyer's drinks expenses | £115.00 |
| Lawyer's car hire | £350.00 |
| Lawyer's chauffeur | £170.00 |
| Lawyer's hairdresser (including £8 tip) | £18.00 |
| Weekend cottage in country for Lawyer and wife (due to stress of case) | £212.00. |

## Credit

| | |
|---|---|
| Gromit's paper round (discontinued) | £20.00 |
| Sold article on 'Edam as a Fashion Accessory' to Woman and Cheese Magazine | £5.00 |
| Won Lottery | £19,000,000 |

Three numbers short. G.    £10.00

| | |
|---|---|
| **Total debits** | £12,042.02 |
| **Total credits** | £37.50 |
| **Net balance** | BROKE. G. |

Chairman's report: Oh dear. Wallace

# THE CHEESE LOVER'S HOROSCOPE

Did you know that your taste in cheese could be influenced by the stars?
This savoury predilection is a vital expression of your personality and has
a significant role to play in your star profile. After all, astrology is governed by the
waxing and waning of the moon – a huge lump of cheese itself! Read this unique
star guide and learn what cheesy morsels you should be eating next year.

**ARIES** *21 March – 19 April*
Personality:    Courageous, active and masterful.
Your Cheese:    Danish blue – a powerful cheese to match
                your forceful nature.

**TAURUS** *20 April – 20 May*
Personality:    Extravagant and pleasure-loving.
Your Cheese:    Any, as long as it's expensive.

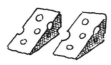

**GEMINI** *21 May – 20 June*
Personality:    Chatty, bright, but split personality.
Your Cheese:    Double Gloucester, or maybe Brie –
                you just can't be pinned down.

**CANCER** *21 June – 22 July*
Personality:    Home-loving, patient and protective.
Your Cheese:    Good old Cheddar – a reliable family
                favourite, just like you!

*Rubbish! Wensleydale's my favourite!*

**LEO** *23 July – 22 August*
Personality:    Noble, strong and dignified.
Your Cheese:    The blue-veined ~~Stilton~~ should appeal to
                someone of your regal stature.

**VIRGO** *23 August – 22 September*

Personality:     Health-conscious and disciplined.

Your Cheese:     With your wholesome lifestyle, you'd better stick to low-fat cheese.

**LIBRA** *23 September – 22 October*

Personality:     Helpful, fair and full of tact.

Your Cheese:     Either ricotta or mozzarella, although it's in the balance.

**SCORPIO** *23 October – 21 November*

Personality:     Intense, desirable and hot-headed.

Your Cheese:     A passionate devil like you won't be able to resist Red Leicester!

**SAGITTARIUS** *22 November – 21 December*

Personality:     A dreamer – deep-thinking and contemplative.

Your Cheese:     Stick to Edam. Anything stronger might give you a headache.

**CAPRICORN** *22 December – 19 January*

Personality:     Resourceful and practical.

Your Cheese:     Goat's cheese – what else?!

**AQUARIUS** *20 January – 18 February*

Personality:     Extremely kind, but also erratic and incomplete.

Your Cheese     Emmental – it's full of holes, but what a wonderful taste.

**PISCES** *19 February – 20 March*

Personality:     Devoted, understanding and fluid.

Your Cheese:     Milky Feta is bound to suit your watery star sign.

# CHEESE MAP OF THE WORLD

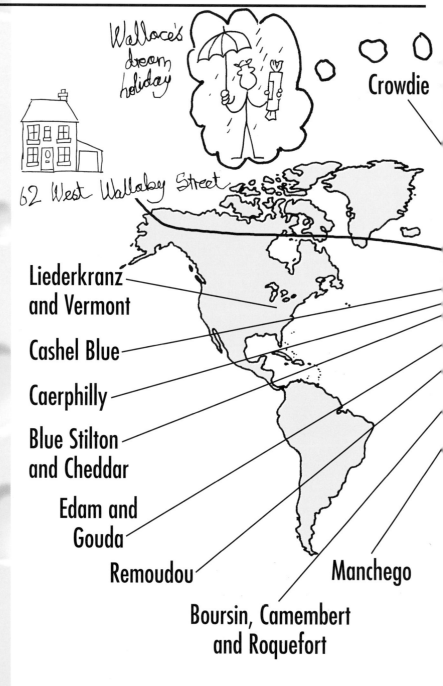

Wallace's dream holiday

Crowdie

62 West Wallaby Street

Liederkranz and Vermont

Cashel Blue

Caerphilly

Blue Stilton and Cheddar

Edam and Gouda

Remoudou

Manchego

Boursin, Camembert and Roquefort

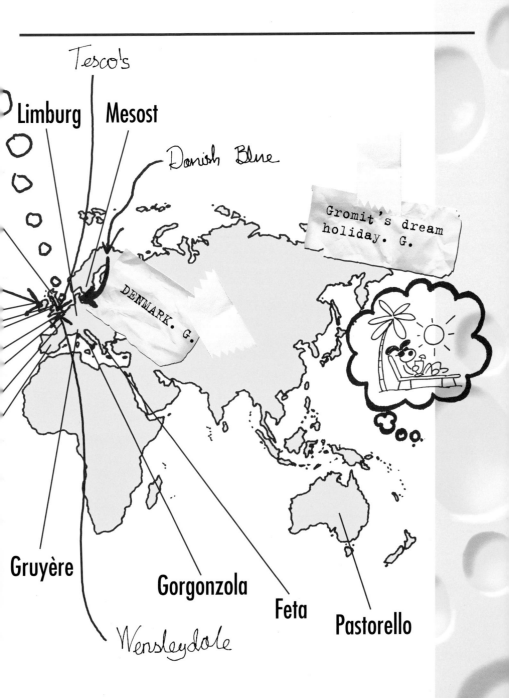

# JANUARY

### CHEESY DIP

Have you ever tried a Dutch Reverse Club Sandwich? Just pop three slices of bread in layers between thick chunks of Edam. It might be a bit of a mouthful, but it's a novel way to ring the changes with your snacks.

**1**

Not sure whether the New Year's Eve party was a good idea. The combination of sherries followed by asti spumante was disastrous – and Gromit was asleep before it was time to see the new year in. Luckily I got off with a warning...

**2**

**3**

Late New Year Resolutions:

Me to design something more than useful
Both of us to eat lots of cheese
Decorate the downstairs toilet
Never drink more than two sherries in one evening.

**4**

Tummy ache. Still trying to finish off the Christmas pudding - it seems a shame to waste it, but if I have another slice I'll spontaneously combust!

Wallace. G.

**5**

**6**

Time for the decorations to come down - the festive season's really over. Always a sad time of year, particularly as I've got to get up that ladder again. We're having a smaller tree next year Gromit, thats for sure!

At least we'll save on the electricity bill - I had to rig up an extra generator to keep the fairy lights going. G.

**7**

# JANUARY

**8**

Back to work lad! Window-cleaning's tough at this time of year, but we've got to make the best of it.

**9**

Got to get Gromit smartened up. I'm entering him for two prizes in the Women's Guild annual pet show on Saturday: 'agility' and the 'most adorable companion' trophies. I think he's quite excited.

no,

No,

NO! G.

**10**

Compulsory day of due to grim weather — we've got to earn some money soon!

Incomings:-
Earnings £38.95 £39.40
Winnings £1.85 £4.85
Insurance claim £4.25
Donations ²65

11.50
39.50
£43.10
£64.10
£39.40

£49.05

Outgoings:-
65.40
4.30
69.70
Bills £69.70
Compensation £38.50
Bribes £3.45
Vet fees £32.85
Cheese bill £54.60
£201.10

**11** Time to examine the Wallaby Street finances.

The piggy bank's empty apart from an old half-crown and a cheese rind. G.

**12**

BIG DAY!

**13** Our champion didn't do so well in the agility, but he came second in the most adorable companion. What a result! We won a deluxe poopa-scoopa and an advanced dog-handling manual.

It's me that needs a Wallace-handling manual. G.

**14** Well done, Gromit!

Big wow, second out of two. G.

2nd Prize

# JANUARY

## CHEESY DIP

Roquefort was discovered when a shepherd in France left a piece of soft sheep's cheese lying next to some bread. Mildew grew all over it, but as he was famished the shepherd ate it just the same and thought it tasted great.

N.B. However, it's not always wise to eat mouldy food, as anyone who has tried other rotten dairy products will tell you...

**15**

Gromit went to bed at seven last night and hasn't spoken since, yesterday - can't understand what's wrong.

**16**

Wish he'd start talking again, I'm just itching to try out the advanced dog-handling manual.

1. D
2. F
3. B
4. Sh

**17**

Friends again! For some reason Gromit took exception to the manual, tore it to pieces! Dogs are strange creatures. Anyway, glad we're pals!

I'm just a big softy. G.

ve
pes o

very da
dient in
nding
is ke

g can be
ld your do
is the

be o
a com
voice
uch mo

**18**

Hit upon a great idea – a recycling machine. Not only will it make us money, it will help save the world.

**19**

MOTORISED RECYC-O-MATIC

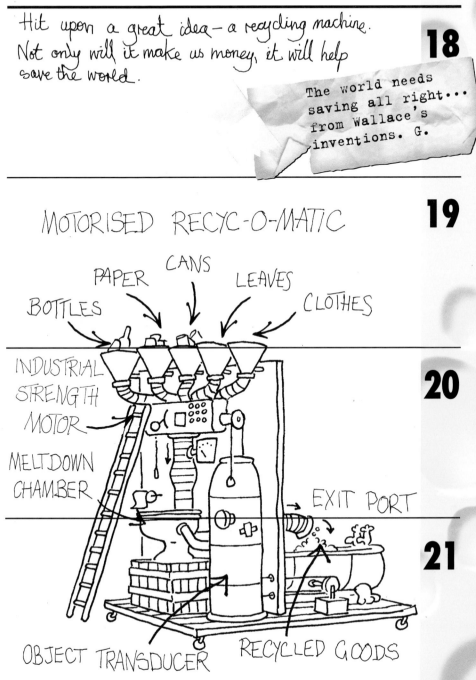

PAPER
CANS
BOTTLES
LEAVES
CLOTHES

**20**

INDUSTRIAL STRENGTH MOTOR

MELTDOWN CHAMBER

EXIT PORT

**21**

OBJECT TRANSDUCER

RECYCLED GOODS

# JANUARY

**22**

RECYC-O-MATIC
Nuts
Bolts
Screws
Wire

**23**   1lb Red Leicester (to keep me going)

**24**   Machine nearing completion — soon I'll be
the talk of the neighbourhood.

That's
what I'm
afraid
of. G.

GERONIMO! The Recyc-O-Matic is in full swing.

Knitting a scarf and gloves for the bring and buy stall — anything to keep away from Wallace's new machine. It worries me. G.

# JANUARY

## CHEESY DIP

In Britain, you could only buy plain crisps until cheese and onion flavour was introduced in 1962. Since then there have been such flavours as Apricot, Chilli with Lemon and Strawberry Fool!

What about Chocolate and Pilchard, Boiled Cabbage and Crème de Porridge?

**29** Added major improvement to the Recyc-O-Matic — a pair of hands. Now it can feed itself which means that I don't have to watch over it all day. Ah, the joys of modern technology

**30**

**31** The Recyc-O Matic has escaped! I left the front door open and it headed out of the house and off towards the town centre. Outside the Town Hall, it snatched up the Mayor's Mercedes and recycled it into two Robin Reliants. Then it seized the entire stock from the window of Doris's Fashion and recycled it into 45 handkerchiefs and a duster. I fear there could be repercussions.

**1**

Recyc-O-Matic found in ditch by side of B4127. Its motor ceased to function — don't know how that could have happened.

**2**

Maintaining a low profile. G.

**3**

Won a giant jar of gooseberry jam at the Hospital Jamboree. Wallace spent the whole afternoon trying not to be recognised. G.

**4**

Gromit's birthday

FEBRUARY

| | | | | |
|---|---|---|---|---|
| Mon - | 05 | 12 | 19 | 26 |
| Tue - | 06 | 13 | 20 | 27 |
| Wed - | 07 | 14 | 21 | 28 |
| Thu 01 | 08 | 15 | 22 | 29 |
| Fri 02 | 09 | 16 | 23 | - |
| Sat 03 | 10 | 17 | 24 | - |
| Sun 04 | 11 | 18 | 25 | - |

# FEBRUARY

**CHEESY DIP**

The French cheese
Baraka is shaped
like a horseshoe.
The name is Arabic
for 'good luck'.

*I could do with some
of that at the moment.*

**5**

**6**

**7**

## TOWN COUNCIL

Environmental Services Dept.
The Town Hall
Red Tape Square

3rd February

Dear Sir,

We have reason to believe that you are the owner of the
mechanical contraption which caused chaos in the town
on 31st January. In the space of thirty minutes, this
machine destroyed the Mayor's official car, devoured
two sets of traffic lights, one traffic warden's uniform
(leaving the warden extremely cold and embarrassed
since he happened to be wearing it at the time),
extensively damaged the frontage of Doris's Fashions
and dug up six prize-winning courgettes on the council
allotments. It also threatened the brass band who were
performing in the Market Place. The tuba player has not
been seen since. You are clearly a menace to society and
will be receiving a bill for this carnage in due course.

Yours sincerely,

*f. Luent*

(Drainage and Highways Division)

**8**

Couldn't decide how to respond and so returned
letter to Council and wrote on an envelope
'NOT KNOWN AT THIS ADDRESS'

**9**

NOTICE TO GROMIT: KEEP OUT
OF THIS DIARY FOR THE
NEXT THREE DAYS. SECRET
PLANS IN DEVELOPMENT.

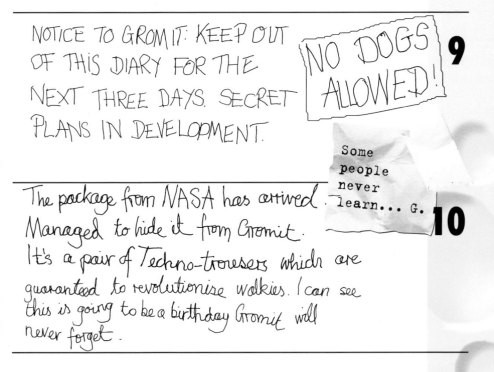

NO DOGS ALLOWED!

Some
people
never
learn... G.

**10**

The package from NASA has arrived.
Managed to hide it from Gromit.
It's a pair of Techno-trousers which are
guaranteed to revolutionise walkies. I can see
this is going to be a birthday Gromit will
never forget.

**11**

All set for Gromit's
big day tomorrow!

# FEBRUARY

## CHEESY DIP

The Romans built a wall around Chester mainly to protect the city's valuable Cheshire cheese industry.

*That's what I call getting your priorities right.*

**12**

What a birthday! Wallace bought me a collar and lead — just what I never wanted — and then produced these scary trousers. I knew he was up to something. Before I could say anything, he had programmed them to drag me to the park and back again. They'll have to go. G.

*I think he liked them.*

**13**

*I think I managed to assemble the trousers correctly. I must say the instructions were pretty complicated even for a technical wizard such as myself*

**14**

*Valentine's day. Gromit and I agreed to send each other an anonymous card so as to avoid undue disappointment.*

# FEBRUARY

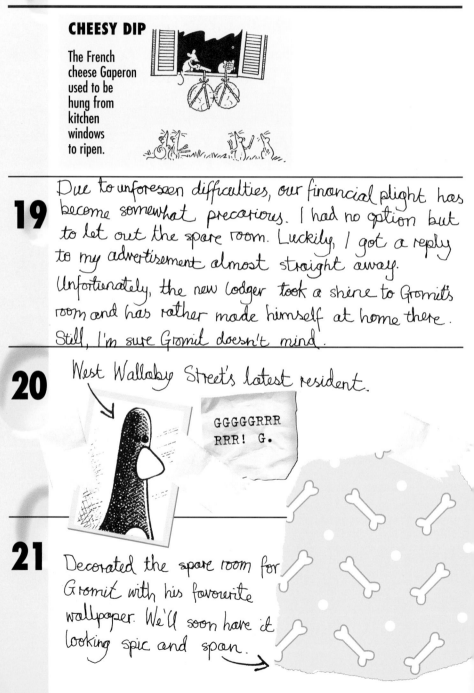

**19** Due to unforeseen difficulties, our financial plight has become somewhat precarious. I had no option but to let out the spare room. Luckily, I got a reply to my advertisement almost straight away. Unfortunately, the new lodger took a shine to Gromit's room and has rather made himself at home there. Still, I'm sure Gromit doesn't mind.

**20** West Wallaby Street's latest resident.

GGGGGRRR RRR! G.

**21** Decorated the spare room for Gromit with his favourite wallpaper. We'll soon have it looking spic and span.

**22**

The lodger likes to keep himself to himself.
He doesn't say much, but I have noticed he
has a bit of a liking for organ music.

The whole street knows he has
a liking for organ music -
particularly at three o'clock
in the morning. I can't stand
it any more. I'm moving out
to the kennel. G.

**23**

What a considerate lodger this penguin is!
He brings me my slippers and the morning
newspaper. He's just like a pet. All things
considered, I thought it only fair to invite
him to partake in supper this evening.

Kennel lacks creature
comforts. Packing bags
and leaving home. G.

The well-oiled breakfast machinery went
horribly wrong when I landed in the
wrong trousers. Before I could enjoy a
nice slice of toast and jam, I found
myself pounding the streets in the
Techno-trousers. They were completely
out of control - I think I'll ask
for my money back.

**25**

Too exhausted to write anything...

# FEBRUARY

## CHEESY DIP

Some cheeses are made from skimmed cow's milk, although no one ever seems to have spotted a skimmed cow.

**26** Crept back home, only to find that the dog-flap had been replaced by a penguin-flap. G.

**27** There's definitely something familiar about that beak. G.

**28** Hope I haven't done anything to offend our lodger - he seems to be avoiding me. I wish he'd give me a hand in trying to remove these wretched Techno-trousers. They're playing havoc with my soft furnishings.

Saw penguin fiddling with trouser control panel and putting a red rubber glove on his head. Feathers McGraw is no chicken! Wonder what he's up to. G.

Two can play at
being masters of
disguise. G.

Woke up to find myself still wearing the
Techno-trousers and hanging from the
ceiling of the City Museum!! It turns
out that our lodger is a fiendish jewel
thief who was using me and the Techno-trousers
to do his dirty work. Thats no way to repay
human kindness, especially as I let him have
an extra cracker at breakfast. Good job
Gromit was on hand to save the day.

**1**

As usual... G.

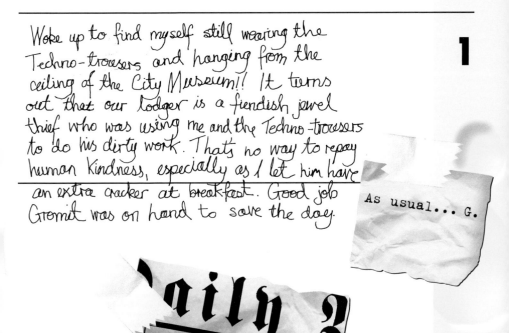

**3**

# MARCH

**CHEESY DIP**

Cornish Yarg is a speciality cheese that is actually served coated in nettles.

**4** Put Techno-trousers in bin.

...along with collar and lead set. G.

**5**

Glad to be back in my room. Must change wallpaper though — it's terrible. G.

**6** At least that rotter McGraw is behind bars, and the £1,000 reward will come in handy. All's well that ends well.

**7**

# HOW I WOULD SPEND £1,000

WALLACE
New pair of slippers
Tea towels  ·· ○ ○ ○ ⬠
Potato peeler – the old
one's getting a bit rusty
New nail clippers

**8**

GROMIT
○ Ferrari (deposit)

A month in Barbados

TV set and video recorder

Flying lessons

Personal CD player (with digital mega bass)

Armani doggie coat

Mediterranean cruise

What's wrong with the wireless then Gromit lad?

**9**

**10**

So that's settled - we'll use the money to pay off outstanding bills and have a spring break caravanning in Budleigh Salterton.

# MARCH

*That sounds exceedingly civil to me*

**CHEESY DIP**

Three hundred tons of Cheshire cheese were sent to Royalist troops in Scotland during the Civil War.

**11** Bathroom tap dripping.

**12** Fixed dripping tap.

**13** Who fixed dripping tap? G.

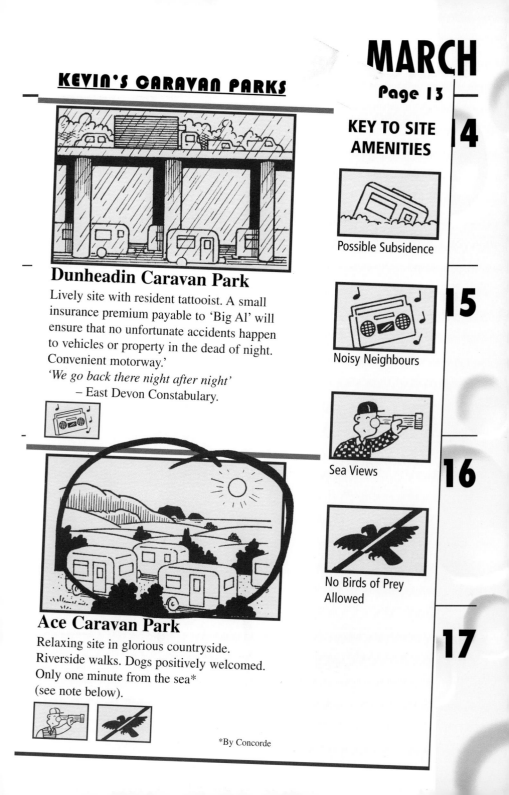

### Dunheadin Caravan Park

Lively site with resident tattooist. A small insurance premium payable to 'Big Al' will ensure that no unfortunate accidents happen to vehicles or property in the dead of night. Convenient motorway.'

*'We go back there night after night'*
    – East Devon Constabulary.

### Ace Caravan Park

Relaxing site in glorious countryside. Riverside walks. Dogs positively welcomed. Only one minute from the sea* (see note below).

*By Concorde

**KEY TO SITE AMENITIES**

Possible Subsidence

Noisy Neighbours

Sea Views

No Birds of Prey Allowed

14

15

16

17

# MARCH

**18** Must remember to attach turbo-thrust recharge generator to motorcycle combination so that it can pull the caravan uphills.

Otherwise I know who would end up pushing. G.

**19** Worked out route that avoids level crossings.

Whenever we go over one, it makes his teeth chatter for the next ten minutes. G.

**20**

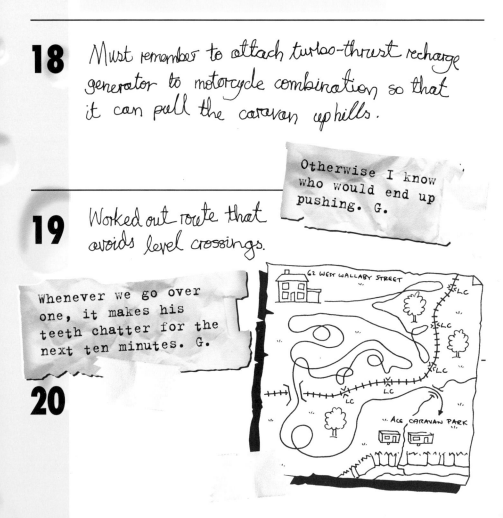

**21**

Went to buy a new pair of bathing trunks. I have a feeling the man in the shop sold me more than I really needed. Still, I'm sure I'll cut quite a dash at the shallow end.

**22**

Cancel milk, newspapers and 'Space Travel for Beginners' magazine. Buy extra cheese for journey.

**23**

Off on holiday.
Wallace's map-
reading let us
down. G.

With motorways and rivers both being blue on the map, it was an easy mistake to make. Anyway we soon dried out.

**24**

Arrived at
caravan
site a day
late. G.

All shops closed.

# MARCH

You'd need a jolly big cracker for that

**25** Built to scale an exact replica of Windsor Castle on beach.

...It looked great. Until the tide came in. G.

**26** Rained.

**27** More rain.
Played I-Spy with Gromit all day.

R for rain featured regularly. G.

# MARCH

## 28

Still
raining. G.

There are 756 flowers on the wallpaper in the caravan.

## 29

A change in the weather at last.

It began
to snow.
G.

## 30

Time to go home. Farewell Budleigh Salterton – thanks for having us.

## 31

# APRIL

**1**

Tried to catch Gromit out by turning the clocks forward an hour and pretending he'd overslept. He didn't fall for it!

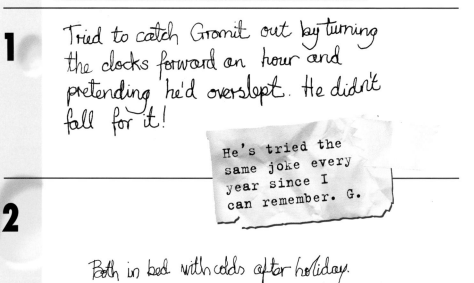

He's tried the same joke every year since I can remember. G.

**2**

Both in bed with colds after holiday.

**3**

**4**

Started making a novelty Easter egg for Gromit – I must be getting better.

I don't like
the sound of
the word
'novelty'. G.

**5**

**6**

Created a bit of a mess with my Easter egg preparations – asked Gromit if he'd pop the duster round tomorrow to clear up. He's such a good lad.

## Radio 4

**6.15. Bone of Contention – Do Dogs Get A Raw Deal From Their Masters?**

Presented by Ken FitzGerald, a wry look at the relationship between man and his best friend.

**7**

Must
remember
to tune
in. G.

# APRIL

Could be
worth a
few days
off
school. G.

**CHEESY DIP**

Why not try making a delicious Easter Egg of chocolate filled with thick, runny cream cheese?

**8**

Must get Gromit to make some cheese pancakes for Easter.

**9**

**10**

SHOPPING LIST FOR PANCAKES

Wensleydale
Eggs
Cheddar
Red Leicester
Flour
Stilton
Lymeswold

Gorgonzola
Neufchatel
Milk
Caerphilly
Single Gloucester
Lemon
Gruyère

**11**

Champion pancakes... although, without wishing to appear critical, I think perhaps they could have done with a little more cheese.

Next year he can make his own. The Fire Brigade still remember the last time he tried. G.

Putting final touches to Gromit's egg - I just know he'll love it!

**13**

Opened Easter egg - from Wallace and six live chicks stepped out of the chocolate. Charming thought, but what am I going to do with them? G.

**14**

# APRIL

## CHEESY DIP

Cheesy Dip: Wensleydale was originally made by Cistercian monks who came over with William the Conqueror in the 11th century. It could have proved a useful weapon at the Battle of Hastings.

**15**

Got our holiday snaps back from chemists:

Say cheese!

**16**

**17**

Having fun in Budleigh Salterton.

What larks!

The people in the next caravan took this.

Must buy
photo
album. G.

# APRIL

*What! Only two mule loads?*

**CHEESY DIP**
King Charlemagne of France was the original cheese lover. He insisted on having two mule loads of Roquefort sent to his palace every single Christmas.

**22**
Spent most of last week trying to round up those Easter chicks I gave Gromit
Having a bit of trouble
– they're lively little chaps.

**23**
Found one sitting in Gromit's favourite chair – the cheek of it!

**24**
Two chicks still missing – using breakfast cereal as bait.

**25**

The pet shop in the High Street announced that there was a half price sale on. I bought Gromit this charming doggie coat.

**26**

He'll be taking that back. G.

**27**

**28**

Finally tracked down the last chick and returned it to the nearest farm.

# APRIL/MAY

**CHEESY DIP**

Blue Cheshire was once used for treating sores and wounds.

A slice of Cheshire always makes me feel better too!

**29** Day out next Bank Holiday? Maybe Sydney, Tokyo or Bridlington. It's a tough choice.

**30** CALAMITY! We're fresh out of cheese! Better go somewhere where we can get new supplies.

238,857 miles (including one-way system in High Street)

**1** Hit upon a great idea. We'll go to the Moon — it's made of cheese. And I hear it's nice there at this time of year.

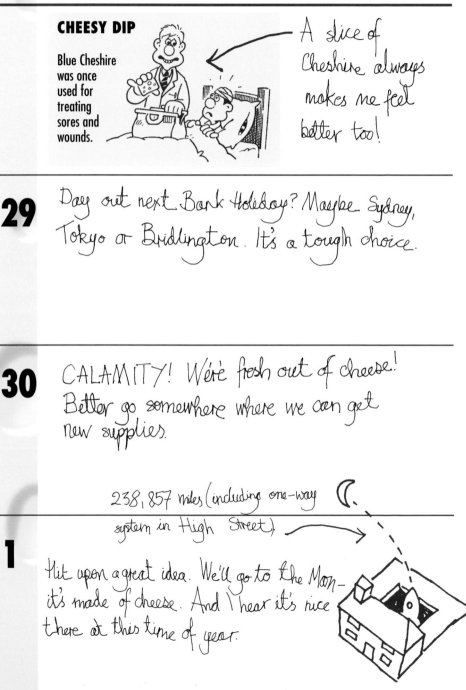

**2**

Spent day in cellar drawing up plans for rocket. Should have it finished in no time at all.

...With a little help from his friends. G.

**3**

Studied 'Electronics for Dogs' all morning. I couldn't understand it, but Gromit seems to know what he is doing.

**4**

Everything on course for lift-off next Monday. Had a few problems with the drill.

**5**

THINGS TO TAKE TO THE MOON

Crackers
Map ✓
⟵ BALL ✓
Picnic hamper ✓
Spanner ✓
~~Sun tan lotion~~ ✓

Box of matches ✓
Camera ✓
Pack of cards ✓

# MAY

**CHEESY DIP**

Cheese was a form of currency in 16th century Denmark and was used to pay church taxes.

'Camembert! That will do nicely.'

**6**

Went to Moon and back. Had a grand day out. Only scare was when we nearly forgot the crackers. It was a nice enough place, although there weren't many people around for a Bank Holiday.

**7**

**8**

Tried some more of the cheese we brought back from the moon. A bit too bland for my liking.

Photos from our trip to the Moon:

I'm afraid it will never replace Wensleydale.

The appliances on the Moon are certainly advanced.

# MAY

### CHEESY DIP

Kefalotiri is called 'head cheese' because it looks like a Greek hat.

**13**

**14**

Finally got through the rest of the Moon cheese. G

**15**

Thought we might try to get some from Mars next year; although first I'll have to phone the ex-NASA store for a few extra parts for the rocket.

**16**

Famous birthday today - Alexander the Cheese Grate.

**17**

Worked out that there is only £2.17 left from our reward money for apprehending Feathers McGraw!

> We better start economising. G.

**18**

Large van parked outside - looks like we've got new neighbours.

**19**

# MAY

**CHEESY DIP**

Smooth and thick with a texture like yoghurt, Quark is Germany's most popular cheese.

It also gets you a good score at Scrabble. G.

## 20

Spoke to the new neighbours today. They seem a nice couple. He says he's a bit of a practical joker. It's always nice to meet people with a sense of humour.

## 21

**BBC 2**

**8.00. CHEESE WATCH**
TV's non-stop broadcast of live churning from Wensleydale.

## 22

Fascinating! Must tune in.

**23**

Finances have hit rock bottom. We've run out of Wensleydale and the Cheddar's gone hard. Whatever are we going to do?

**24**

There's one thing for it – I've got to come up with a money-spinner.

**25**

Wallace has walled himself up in the basement. I'm worried – he must be thinking. Better keep "Electronics for Dogs" on hand just in case. G.

**26**

You reeker! A great idea. I'm on the scent at last. Where's my drawing board?

Uh oh. G.

# MAY

*Great! Just what I've been looking for to seal the pipes.*

## CHEESY DIP

Why not have a go at fondue? It's a kind of hot soup made out of melted Gruyère cheese and wine. Dunk lumps of bread into this delicious mixture for a fabulous Swiss meal. Warning: Always serve this piping hot, because Gruyère is a stretchy cheese that will cool down into an undelectable sort of rubber.

**27**

**28**

**29**

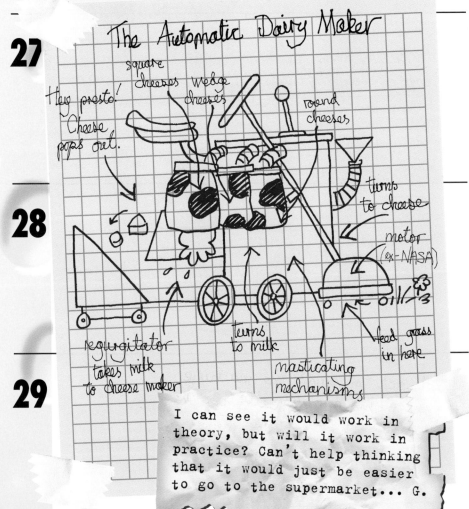

The Automatic Dairy Maker

Hey presto! Cheese pops out.

square cheeses

wedge cheeses

round cheeses

turns to cheese

motor (ex-NASA)

feed grass in here

regurgitator takes milk to cheese maker

turns to milk

masticating mechanisms

I can see it would work in theory, but will it work in practice? Can't help thinking that it would just be easier to go to the supermarket... G.

Off to the scrap-heap this afternoon
to find an old lawn-mower and
washing machine. Better check
that the motorbike and
sidecar's ready to go.

**30**

Had to break the
piggy bank to buy the
materials, so hope
this is worth it. G.

**31**

**1**

All set to build the machine
now - this could really be the
big one (think of the money
we'll save on Wensleydale!)

**2**

# JUNE

### CHEESY DIP

Why not try Double
Gloucester Old Spot,
a distinctive new cheese
made from pigs' milk?
Noted for its firm rind.

Cracking crackling!

**3** Hard at work on Automatic Dairy Maker.
Finished just in time for the shipping
forecast on the wireless. They're having a
rough time of it in Cromarty, Dogger and
German Bite.

**4**

**5** Tested Automatic Dairy Maker in front
garden. Only one minor hitch.... and the
man from the council said next door's
wall would have fallen down soon anyway.

**6**

Gromit has decided to call our cheese 'Creamy Wallaby'. I think that sums up the flavour nicely.

**7**

## CHEESE FOR EUROPE COMPETITION

Calling budding cheesemakers! This is your last chance to enter the competition to create a new cheese for Europe. First prize is a grand day out at Cheddar Gorge.

All entrants should send a photograph of themselves together with a slice of their cheese to: A Cheese For Europe, Nilpoints Hall, London WC1 3GG. Closing date 12th June.

Must enter.

Another competition. G.

**8**

Entering cheese in Gromit's name — he deserves it.

**9**

2.00 Told Gromit to have a bath — he must look his best for photos.

# JUNE

**CHEESY DIP**

For an unusual holiday treat, why not try cheese flavoured ice cream this summer?

**10**

Took Gromit to photobooth. Results interesting.

**11**

Kept fingers crossed as I sent off slice of Creamy Wallaby. This made posting the parcel difficult.

**12**

The waiting is unbearable. I'm nervous wreck.

**EVENING POST** 13

## CHEESE STRAW POLL MAKES GROMIT FAVOURITE

14

*YIPPEE! WE'VE WON!*

15

16

*By way of celebration, rushed out and bought a bottle of dandelion and burdock and a large slice of Wensleydale.*

*VERY FIZZY*

# JUNE

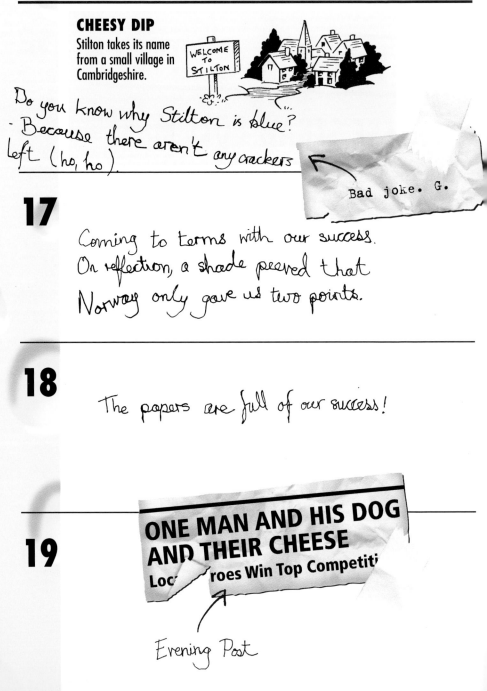

## CHEESY DIP

Stilton takes its name from a small village in Cambridgeshire.

WELCOME TO STILTON

Do you know why Stilton is blue?
- Because there aren't any crackers
left (ho, ho).

Bad joke. G.

**17**

Coming to terms with our success.
On reflection, a shade peeved that
Norway only gave us two points.

**18**

The papers are full of our success!

**19**

ONE MAN AND HIS DOG
AND THEIR CHEESE
Loc... ...roes Win Top Competiti...

Evening Post

## WHAT A CRACKER!

### DOG IN CHEESE SENSATION

The winner of magazine *Cheese Quarterly*'s competition to create a new cheese for Europe.

### Cheesed Off! Irish Eyes Aren't Smiling

A heated row has broken out over a European competition to create a new cheese for Europe.

The Globe

**22**

Our prayers have been answered! Creamy Wallaby is so well known we'll be able to manufacture it for the cheese-loving public!

**23**

I hope he isn't getting carried away... G.

# JUNE

**24**

Received a phone call asking us to appear on breakfast television to talk about Creamy Wallaby. Had to turn it down, they wouldn't let me bring my own toaster.

**25**

● New Edam

**26**

6.00 Interview for The Cheese Programme, Radio Bristol.

# CHEESE BOARD

25 June

Dear Gromit,
    Following your success in our competition to find A CHEESE FOR EUROPE, I am pleased to inform you that you have won two tickets to Cheddar Gorge on 5th July when you will be presented with your trophy. I would have looked forward to meeting you then, but I've got a game of golf arranged for that day.

Yours fairly sincerely.

*A. E. Butterworth*

(chairman)

A letter from the head of the board — the big cheese himself!

# JULY

## CHEESY DIP

The most popular vegetarian dish is cauliflower cheese, made with baked cauliflower and grated cheese.

Better still, forget the cauliflower

**1**

Must be extra nice to Gromit so that he'll take me with him to Cheddar.

Wonder who I can take. G.

**2**

Took Gromit breakfast in bed.

Still haven't decided who to take with me. G.

**3**

Allowed Gromit to sit in my favourite chair and then even let him take me for a walk.

**4**

Gromit says he's taking me on the trip to Cheddar! That's an offer I can't refuse.

**5**

Good, because marriage is out of the question. G.

A splendid day out at Cheddar Gorge with grand food. I had the ploughman's lunch – I don't think he was particularly pleased.

**6**

◑ Half-way through the Edam

OUR FINEST HOUR

MY. G.

**7**

THE WINNERS!

CHEESE FOR EUROPE

# JULY

### CHEESY DIP

The most popular English and Welsh cheese is Cheddar, followed by Cheshire and Red Leicester.

Apparently Wensleydale only comes seventh. It's a scandal — I demand a recount.

**8**

**9**

Sales of Creamy Wallaby ticking along nicely.

**10** Made another £4.40 today. I don't even mind getting up at the crack of dawn.

Speak for yourself. G.

**11**

○ Finished Edam

**12**

Dear Wallace,
   (and not forgetting Gromit!)

Having a super fortnight in the
Amazonian jungle. I can cope with
the snakes, the alligators and the heat,
but the only problem is you can't get
a decent bit of Cheddar out here to
save your life. See you when I get back.

   Regards,

   Vernon Hoole
      (Cheese Society)

Wallace
62 West Wallaby Street
ENGLAND

**1st**

**13**

**14**

Imagine having to go two weeks without cheese—
it doesn't bear thinking about!

# JULY

**15**

**16**

Hard at work selling Creamy Wallaby.

**17**

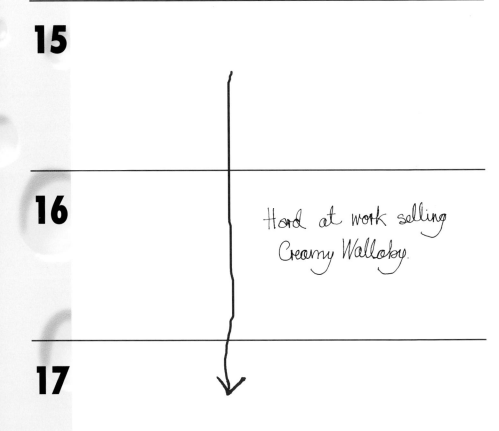

# JULY

**18**

It's still going like hot cakes.

**19**

**20**

In danger of running
out of stock!

**21**

Too exhausted to
get excited. G.

# JULY

### CHEESY DIP

In the 12th century, Blanche of Navarre tried to win the heart of French King Philippe Auguste by sending him 200 cheeses each year.

**22** DISASTER! All stocks of Creamy Wallaby have been repossessed. Apparently some people had a bad reaction to the grass ingredient.

**23**

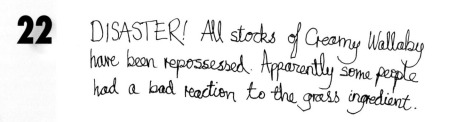

## HOW GREEN IS MY VALET
### Servant's Grassy Rash

**24** Gromit's cheese has really landed us in a pickle.

So suddenly it's _my_ cheese... G.

**25**

Had to return all Creamy Wallaby earnings so back in dire financial straits.

At least we managed to
go to Cheddar Gorge
with this invention. G.

**26**

**27**

USED DIARY TO BALANCE
WOBBLY TABLE

**28**

Due to pressure to compensate for money lost recently, have decided to put the window-cleaning business on a more commercial footing.

# JULY

**CHEESY DIP**
The ancient French cheese Maroilles is so pungent that it is known affectionately as 'old stinker'.

**29**

Only nine days to my birthday. Wonder what Gromit's got lined up by way of a surprise.

**30**

Picked up some nice Camembert from Ye Olde Cheese Shoppe. Unfortunately the prices were all too modern.

**31**

Currently focussing all my attention on perfecting my window-cleaning equipment.

> Surely we could just use a bucket and sponge like everyone else? G.

**1**

I'm sure Gromit's planning something special for my birthday. Perhaps it's a big party with members of the local Cheese Society?

Nope. G.

**2**

**3**

**4**

I reckon Gromit's planning a birthday trip to the cinema to see 'A Cheese Called Gouda'.

Try again. G.

# AUGUST

**CHEESY DIP**

Here's a handy tip. Why not use a slab of Emmental as a pencil holder?

**5**

With gift ideas such as this, I'm never short of friends.

**6**

The day before my birthday! Can't wait to see what Gromit's got in store for me tomorrow !!

**7**

Had a quiet evening in.

# AUGUST

What a rascal! Just when I thought he'd forgotten my birthday, Gromit presented me with a vintage packet of limited edition crackers. They're from 1948 - one of the finest years. It's the best present I've ever had!

**8**

**9**

**10**

Can't wait to try one of my crackers. I wonder how they'll taste after all these years.

The doctor says I should be O.K. in a day or two.

**11**

Sorry. G.

# AUGUST

It was a shame they had to dash back to Britain to fetch the crackers.

**CHEESY DIP**
A 1956 expedition to the South Pole found a tin of Edam left behind by Scott and his team in 1912. The cheese was still fit to eat.

**12** Plans coming along nicely.

**13** WINDOW-CLEANING DEVICES

ME

GROMIT

What a surprise. G.

**14** Must think of a catchy name for the business — what about WALLACE AND GROMITS AUTOMATED WINDOW-CLEANSING POLISHING AND DRYING SERVICE?

**15**

HAVE SPONGE, WILL TRAVEL

~~WINDYCLEAN LTD~~

~~ICI~~

DOPE ON A ROPE

WALLACE AND GROMIT'S
WASH 'N' GO

*Window-cleaning Service*

G.

**16**

Work out local newspaper advertisement.
Need to imply trust – if we miss a window, we
don't expect to get paid.

**17**

No pane,
no gain.
G.

**18**

# AUGUST

**19** Made business sign for front garden.

**20**

**21** I dare say the phone will soon be red hot with prospective customers.

**Beautiful wedding dress for sale.** Only used for going to shops. 1.6 litre engine. Room for 4 people. Damaged rear light, slight rust under rims. One careful owner.

**Second-hand Austin Maestro. Complete with sun-roof.** Net underskirt, floral headband and lace veil, kept in a box on top of wardrobe for 40 years. £30 o.n.o.

**Wallace & Gromit's Wash 'n' Go Window Cleaning Service.** Reliable, friendly service. Competitive rates. Have own bucket and ladder. Telephone 2143.

**Tree fellers – Mick, Paddy and Seamus.** Will take care of all your garden needs. Ring 8172.

# AUGUST

**CHEESY DIP**
Dunlop cheese gets its name from the town in Scotland where it was first made, not because it tastes like a rubber tyre. It is important not to get the two Dunlops confused.

**26**   NO CALLS

**27**   Waited by the telephone all day – just in case.

**28**   Asked telephone company to check that all equipment was in working order. The gentleman on the other end was exceedingly pleasant and persuaded me to join a scheme which would give me cheap-rate calls to Cuba in July (after midnight). He also sold me a visual display unit, a callback modem amplifier and a special bone-shaped receiver for Gromit. I'm sure all of these things will come in really useful. As for checking for faults, he said they'd try and get round some time in November.

Decided to take a look at the cables myself.

**29**

Big
mistake. G.

**30**

**31**

Decided to leave telephone repairs to the experts

The telephone rang - it was a wrong number.

**1**

# SEPTEMBER

### CHEESY DIP

The French Emperor Napoleon Bonaparte was a fan of Époisses, a soft cheese with a tangy flavour.

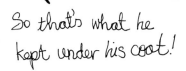

So that's what he kept under his coat!

## 2

Late last night I heard a lorry outside. Made me drop a stitch. G.

## 3

Not a good start to the day. Porridge cannon seriously malfunctioned, leaving me with egg on my face – not to mention porridge. Looks as if something has been chewing the wiring. On the plus side, we were requested to clean the windows of Wendolene's Wools in the High Street. I have to admit I was quite taken with the charming proprietor, Wendolene Ramsbottom. She even had a nice dog for Gromit to play with.

## 4

Discovered why everything in the house was being systematically chewed. It was the work of a stray lamb. Cleaned him up in the Knit-O-Matic machine and soon had him looking as good as new. Decided to name the lamb Shaun – he's a cute little chap.

**5**

While Gromit was washing the town hall clock, I took the opportunity to visit the fair Wendolene, but I'd only said hello when I was swept out of the shop on a tidal wave of sheep.

**6**

EVENING POST SEPTEMB

**7**

What a terrible day! The house is full of sheep and Gromit has been arrested for killing one of their number. Can't help feeling he's really let the side down this time.

**8**

Wendolene called round to apologise, but I'm not too sure what she was apologising for. Women can be a mystery sometimes.

# SEPTEMBER

**CHEESY DIP**

When the ill-fated Louis XVI was seized in 1792 during the French Revolution, he told his captors that all he wanted was 'a glass of red wine and a piece of Brie'.

**9** These sheep are eating me out of house and home – they're even polished off the last of the crackers.

**10** And the wrapper.

**11** And the pedal bin. Can't sleep at night because I'm too busy counting sheep.

**SHEEP DOG TRIAL CONTINUES**

**12**

Daily Beagle SEPTEMBER 13TH

**GROMIT BIT ME, SAYS SHEPHERD**

**13**

STOP PRESS...STOP PRESS

**GROMIT FOUND GUILTY**

**14**

EXCLUSIVE INTERVIEW WITH POLICE

**GROMIT GETS LIFE**

roke out in ... ...ay after Judge Chapman Q.C

**15**

Looks like I'll never see him again.

Goodbye, old friend.

# SEPTEMBER

**CHEESY DIP**

Gruyère is a
flavoursome,
holey Swiss
delight made
with full milk.

Don't forget
to book
dentists
appointment.

## 16

The sheep are certainly making themselves at at home.

## 17

## 18

of Bach's Toccata in D minor and an interview
with contemporary composer Joanna Smith.

**Radio 4**

**7.30.  Pedigree Chums: What
Happens When Your Dog Is
Sent To Jail**

An insightful documentary into the effects on
humans when a canine family member turns
out to be a criminal.

**19**

10pm Shaun said we were off to see Gromit in prison — it seemed a little late for visiting time. The next thing I knew I was helping him escape! What a relief to get the lad out safe and sound.

**20**

What a night! It turned out that Wendolene's dog, Preston, was no ordinary pet but a CYBERDOG!! And he'd been rustling sheep and turning them into cans of dog food with Wendolene as his helpless accomplice. We had quite a chase in the motorcycle combination — touching 35mph at one point — and

**21**

thanks to Shaun and Gromit, Preston ended up a victim of his own dastardly Mutton-O-Matic machine.

Relieved to have come out of this
in one piece.

Instead of several
hundred, like
Preston. G.

**22**

# SEPTEMBER

**CHEESY DIP**

The French cheese Brillat Savarin was named after the man who said 'a meal without cheese is like a beautiful woman with only one eye'.

It's not a simile I would have used myself, but I agree with the sentiments.

**23** It's so good to have Gromit back—now we're a proper family again.

**24**

SHAUN TOOK THIS

**25** Spent the afternoon rebuilding Preston — it took ages to find all the bits to put him back together again. Quite pleased with the finished result, he shouldn't give Wendolene any trouble now.

**26**

Wendolene popped round with Preston II. But when I asked her whether she would care to step inside for some cheese, she politely declined, saying it brings her out in a rash. Must say I was a bit disappointed.

**27**

**Daily Beag—**

**GROMIT EXONERATED**

Today's leading story is the exoneration of Gromit the d—

**28**

And not before time. G.

**29**

Gromit has persuaded me to let Shaun stay with us for a while — I hope I don't live to regret it.

# SEPTEMBER/OCTOBER

### CHEESY DIP

One of Italy's oldest cheeses, Gorgonzola is famous for the bluey green veins which run through it.

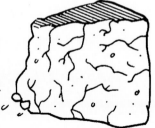

**30** Shaun has eaten my favourite pair of slippers, the hall carpet and part 173 of 'Space Travel for Beginners', not to mention a whole packet of Wensleydale.

He's just pining for his friends. G.

**1**

**2** Can't get Wendolene out of my mind. There's something about her - that hair, that smile...

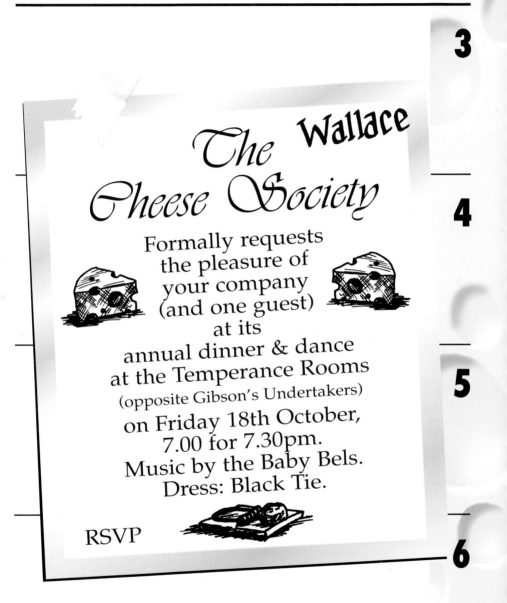

## The Wallace Cheese Society

Formally requests
the pleasure of
your company
(and one guest)
at its
annual dinner & dance
at the Temperance Rooms
(opposite Gibson's Undertakers)
on Friday 18th October,
7.00 for 7.30pm.
Music by the Baby Bels.
Dress: Black Tie.

RSVP

# OCTOBER

## CHEESY DIP

Doncaster Crust is a relative newcomer to the world of cheese. A highly pungent variety, it is guaranteed to keep you warm and awake on those chilly autumn nights.

Mmm. It really does capture the taste of Doncaster.

---

**7**

Plucking up the courage to ask Wendolene to the dinner and dance. Must get on with it soon because faint heart never won fair lady.

Or Wendolene. G.

---

**8**

Telephoned Wendolene. We talked about the weather for half an hour.

Poor Wallace - I haven't seen him looking so nervous since the National Cracker Strike. G.

---

**9**

Fortified by a hearty cheese supper, I telephoned Wendolene again and popped the question, so to speak. Assured her that she wouldn't have to actually eat cheese. She said she would have loved to have gone to the dinner and dance but it clashes with a wool convention in Harrogate.

WALLACE. G.

Gromit tried to cheer me up with a game of Donkey. I ended up with the donkey.

**10**

Shaun brought me a book to cheer me up.

**11**

Stayed in bed

**12**

Me – a broken man.

Wonderful news! Wendolene called to say that her convention has been cancelled. She can go to the ball!

**13**

# OCTOBER

## CHEESY DIP

American Brick cheese is so named because it is made in the shape of a brick. This can cause confusion to those non-acquainted with the delicacy.

**14** Hired my dinner suit.

> He looks suspiciously like a penguin in it. G.

**15**

**16** Gromit has kindly agreed to babysit Preston II on Friday.

> Did I have a choice? G.

**17**

Collected Wendolene's posy. Hope she's not allergic to carnations as well as cheese.

Bought magnet to keep Preston II under control. G.

**18**

Evening was a great success - We danced till gone 9.30.

**19**

**20**

# OCTOBER

### CHEESY DIP

When spread on oatcakes, the Scottish cheese Crowdie used to be known as 'cruddy butter'. It was particularly popular before a ceilidh as it was believed to limit the effects of extensive whisky drinking.

'Where's the cruddy butter.'

## 21

Must tidy up the garden in case Wendolene pops round. In fact, it's the perfect opportunity to try out my new Push-Button Gardener.

## 22

___

## 23

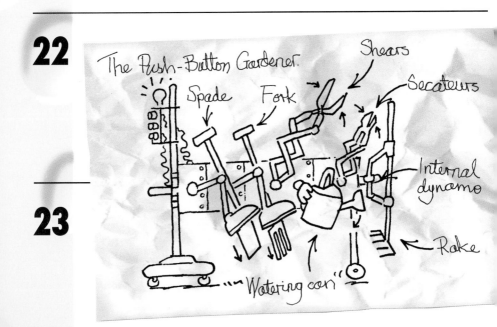

The Push-Button Gardener.

Spade — Fork — Shears — Secateurs — Internal dynamo — Rake — "Watering can"

**24**

That gardening machine did a grand job raking up the leaves.

Before dumping them on the living-room carpet. G.

**25**

More work needed on the Push-Button Gardener.

**26**

Sheffield Wensleydale were playing at home so Gromit and I went along to support the team. Unfortunately we lost 2-1 to Colcheddar United.

**27**

# OCTOBER

### CHEESY DIP

This week's handy tip is for Edam jack o'lanterns. Why go to the trouble of hollowing out pumpkins for Hallowe'en when you could create much more scrumptious de-lights from carved Edams?

N.B. Beware of melting.

**28**

**29** Gromit and I intend going trick-or-treating.

**30** Gromit and I in our costumes. Funny eh?!

**31**

Gave Wendolene a real surprise with our trick-or-treat costumes. Preston II took quite a fancy to me but I managed to shake him off by the end of the street.

**1**

**2**

The garden still looks a mess - I've decided that it's the Push-Button Gardener's day off.

Built a kennel for Shaun now that the nights are drawing in. G.

**3**

SHAUN

SHEEP DIP

# NOVEMBER

## CHEESY DIP

What could be better as a reviving Bonfire Night snack than the classic jacket potato smothered in Cheddar cheese.

**4**

Dressed Shaun up as a guy. G.

We managed to collect 77p, three paper clips and a button. G.

**5**

Attended Grand Firework Display in park. Wendolene was there too - our eyes met across a Chrysanthemum Fountain.

**6**

SPACE TRAVEL FOR BEGINNERS    PAGE 2

# WIN A TRIP TO MARS

Bored with your everyday routine? Tired of your humdrum existence? You can win a fantastic trip to Mars just by sending in three wrappers from Armitage's Baked Beans and by completing the slogan below in your own words (maximum words allowed 20)

"I would like to go to Mars because..."

Closing date 12th November. Must be over 15 to enter. This competition is being run in association with Armitage's Baked Beans – "the beans astronauts prefer."

"I would like to go to Mars because...."
I want to travel and meet people.
I'm sure the cheese up there's delicious.
I could pop in and see my friends on Jupiter.
There's nothing much on the wireless tonight.

# NOVEMBER

## CHEESY DIP

The ancient sport of cheese-rolling takes place each year on a steep hill in Gloucestershire. Local youngsters run down the hill and try to catch a 7lb circular Double Gloucester cheese before it reaches the bottom.

**11** Sent off the Mars competition form – I think we could be on to another winner.

I won't pack my case just yet... G.

**12** That gardening machine is driving me crazy! This afternoon it tore out every single winter pansy in the front border and decimated the compost heap.

We've just got to try and catch it first. G.

**13** Have reached the end of the road with that wretched Push-Button Gardener. Have finally arranged for it to be taken away for good. The scrap metal merchant is coming round at seven.

14

15

16

17

# NOVEMBER

### CHEESY DIP

Try out this great recipe for Victoria Sponge Surprise. Simply bake your spongecakes as normal then fill them with generous lashings of cream cheese instead of strawberry jam. This ingenious twist on a culinary classic is sure to transform any tea party.

**18** What an ordeal!! Spent all of the last few days trying to deactivate the Gardener. It took longer to pull apart than it did to invent!

**19** Had better put inventing on hold for a while.

Like ten years. G.

**20**

**21**

Didn't win the competition. The winning slogan was "I would like to go to Mars because I would be able to introduce a whole new planet to the joys of Armitage's Baked Beans".

**22**

Wish I'd thought of that. G.

**23**

On our way to a window-cleaning assignment, the clutch broke on the motorcycle combination, leaving us stranded in the High Street. It was a messy job, but Gromit managed to fix it. What a clever dog he is!

**24**

Wish you'd always leave the technical stuff to me - it would be a lot safer. G.

# NOVEMBER

### CHEESY DIP

Wensleydale is often eaten with apple pie, a point illustrated by the old Yorkshire rhyme 'Apple pie without cheese/Is like a kiss without a squeeze.'

Must remember to recite that to Wendolene at an opportune moment.

**25** LETTER TO SANTA (first draft, to be written up in best later.)

To: Santa Claus, P.O. Box 1312, Lapland, Somewhere north of Sweden.

Dear Santa,
What with one thing and another, it has been a hectic sort of year and as such therefore, I must apologise profusely for not thanking you hitherto for the personalised cheese grater you

**26** sent my way last Christmas. Notwithstanding my regular request for a cheese selection box, the present I would really like this year is the hand of a lady acquaintance of mine, the beautiful Wendolene, who owns the wool shop in the High Street (There is a sale on at the moment if you are interested). I appreciate that affairs of the heart are probably outside your usual jurisdiction, but any assistance would be greatly appreciated.

**27** Yours Faithfully,
Yours truly,
Yours sincerely
Kindest Regards,

Wallace
P.S. I have eaten all my greens this year.

Dear Santa,

For Christmas I would like 'A Dog's Guide to the Theory of Relativity', 'The Complete Works of Chaucer', 'Rachmaninov's Second Piano Concerto', a signed photo of Beethoven (the dog) and a big juicy bone. Hope this list is not too long.

Yours,

Gromit

DeAr SaNTa

BAAAAH
ShaUn

# DECEMBER

**2**

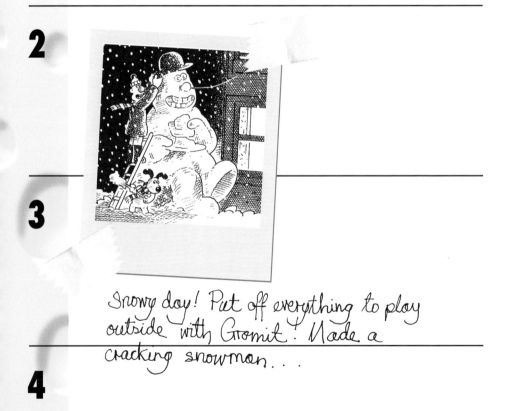

**3**

Snowy day! Put off everything to play
outside with Gromit! Made a
cracking snowman...

**4**

**5**

# SANTA GETS THE SACK

Thousands of local children face a heartbreaking Christmas because the Alderman Crippen Leisure Centre has no Santa. The crisis occurred after the previous Santa, a bit of a practical joker, was dismissed on Friday for supergluing two children to his sleigh and for detonating stink bombs in the grotto. Earlier in the week, the actor playing Rudolf was sent home suffering from nervous exhaustion. Anyone able to take over the role of Santa should ring 3360.

The centre has also announced that next week's hypochondriacs' self-help group has been cancelled due to sickness.

I think I might apply - anything to **6** bring about a spot of yuletide cheer.

**7**

And it might impress Wendolene.

2.00 Interview at leisure centre. Fingers crossed.

And paws. G. **8**

# DECEMBER

## CHEESY DIP

Stilton is such a valued savoury delicacy, it is the only British cheese which is protected by law.

**9** Leisure centre telephoned to say I've got the job as Santa. Practised my finest HO! HO! HO!

**10** Tried on costume. It was definitely big enough.

Haven't heard from Wendolene for a few days – perhaps she's not a big fan of Father Christmas.

**11** First day at the grotto. The children were certainly high-spirited. It went quite well – all things considering. And as I told the manager, it wasn't a full-scale riot.

## 12

## Cheese Society

On Tuesday 17th December at 8pm,

### a Cheese and Whine Evening

will be held for those who wish to
air their grievances about the running
of the Cheese Society.

Ready to face another day at the grotto—
the pills the doctor prescribed seem to
be working. Still no word from Wendolene.

Hovered outside wool shop for two
hours, hoping to catch a glimpse of
Wendolene. The shop seemed shut.

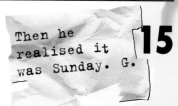

Then he realised it was Sunday. G.

# DECEMBER

**CHEESY DIP**

Mild and delicate Derby cheese is traditionally stored bound in cloth.

Sometimes I prefer to wrap mine in an old string vest. It allows the cheese to breathe.

**16**

Wendolene called round last night – she had been busy with Christmas orders and having her hair re-styled. I certainly like her new look.

??? G.

**17**

Think I'll give the Cheese Society meeting a miss – it sounds too confrontational for my taste.

**18**

# DECEMBER

**19**

Invented a Stuff-O-Matic automatic stuffing machine to take the pain out of preparing Christmas dinner.

1. SAGE AND ONION
2. THYME AND PARSLEY
3. SAUSAGE MEAT
4. CHESTNUT AND APPLE
5. QUADRUPLE GLOUCESTER

**20**

Put up the Christmas tree, it looked so lovely I had to take one for the album.

It's a shame we couldn't find the fairy.

**21**

Busy day at the grotto – I came home with four bruises, a heavily-bandaged ankle and a cut lip. Boys will be boys.

**22**

Took Wendolene her present – A £10 supermarket token.

# DECEMBER

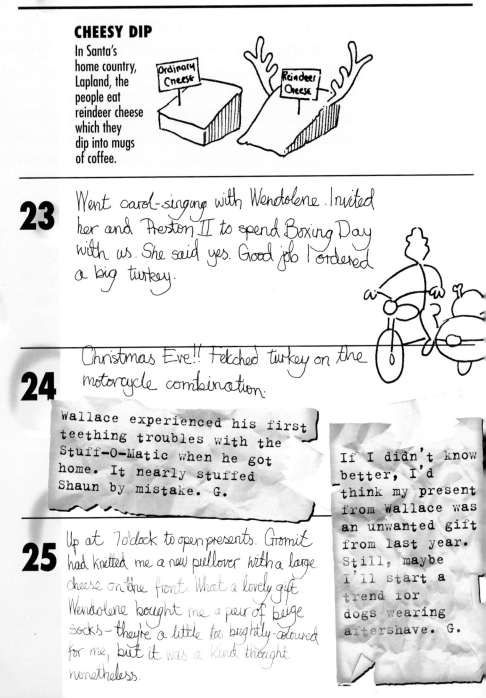

**23** Went carol-singing with Wendolene. Invited her and Preston II to spend Boxing Day with us. She said yes. Good job I ordered a big turkey.

**24** Christmas Eve!! Fetched turkey on the motorcycle combination.

Wallace experienced his first teething troubles with the Stuff-O-Matic when he got home. It nearly stuffed Shaun by mistake. G.

If I didn't know better, I'd think my present from Wallace was an unwanted gift from last year. Still, maybe I'll start a trend for dogs wearing aftershave. G.

**25** Up at 7 o'clock to open presents. Gromit had knitted me a new pullover with a large cheese on the front. What a lovely gift. Wendolene bought me a pair of beige socks — they're a little too brightly-coloured for me, but it was a kind thought nonetheless.

# DECEMBER

**26**

A most cordial day with Wendolene and Preston II. Played Happy Families in the afternoon – until Shaun ate Mr Bun the Baker. Cold turkey for lunch, turkey sandwiches for tea.

**27**

Gromit was a whiz in the kitchen. He made turkey soup for lunch, turkey on toast for tea, followed by ice cream surprise.

The surprise was it was turkey-flavoured. G.

**28**

Wendolene's birthday! She came and joined me for a romantic dinner (Turkey risotto).

**29**

Hurrah! The last of the turkey. G.

# DECEMBER/JANUARY

### CHEESY DIP

To allow the growth of the mould which gives many blue cheeses their colour, needles are inserted into the cheese.

'Keep still, this won't hurt!'

---

**30** Went ice skating with Gromit.

> It reminded me of Bambi on ice. G.

Found uneaten leg of turkey under Gromit's pillow. Made him eat it for tea.

---

**31** Decided to see the New Year in quietly at home.

> Filled all the sherry bottles with Vimto — he'll never notice. G.

---

**1**

> Shattered. After a dull evening I spent the whole night awake listening to the neighbours enjoying themselves at a party next door. G.

Yes, in hindsight we should have thought of a more exciting way of celebrating than spending the night in (even the sherry tasted a bit off).

**2**

NEW YEAR'S RESOLUTIONS
— WALLACE
Eat more cheese
~~Discover a new civilization~~
Finish jigsaw in attic.
Ask for Wendolene's hand in marriage
Repair alarm clock.
Be more decisive?

**3**

```
GROMIT
Be more
patient
with dumb
humans. G.
```

**4**

Last Entry — how time's flown by. I've got
high hopes for next year — I really think I'm
going to make it as a serious inventor....

**5**

```
That means I've got my work
cut out for the foreseeable
          future. G.
```

# NOTES

Cheese – Wensleydale (in bulk from Tesco's)
Crackers
Milk
Jam
Notebook (for my inventions)
White loaf
Extra cheese
Fresh tea
New 2" spanner (broke the last one dismantling the Push-Button Gardener)
Armitage baked beans
10 yards of cable (to replace wiring Shaun chewed through)
Butter
Oats

Back-up supplies. G.

Porridge cannon running low. G.

# NOTES

## CHEESE ON A ROPE
The perfect Christmas gift!

Mail order only:
21, The High Street, Bridlington.

### Slipper Repairs
*"No Job Too Small"*
Call 3881

Cobblers. G.

### INVENTION CONVENTION
Annual meeting for all serious inventors, held at the Science Museum, London. Attendees are welcome to bring along their more serious creations for public exhibition. Tickets available now for next year's convention on 3rd June.

*Already booked a place for me and Gromit.*

I thought you might have! G.

### Tank Top Man
Specialist in quality tank tops for the discerning dresser.
23 North Road Cleethorpes
Telephone 2227

# INVENTIONS

Wallace's emergency quick tea pourer.

For when those surprise guests pop around.

**Jet Slipper**
- 1 foot
- Air intake
- Fuel
- Jet

**Roller Slipper**
- 1 foot
- Roller blades

**Roller Rocket Slipper**
- 1 foot
- Toe cap for fuel
- Roller blades
- Rocket
- Jet

**Spring Jumper Slipper**
- 1 foot
- Bed springs

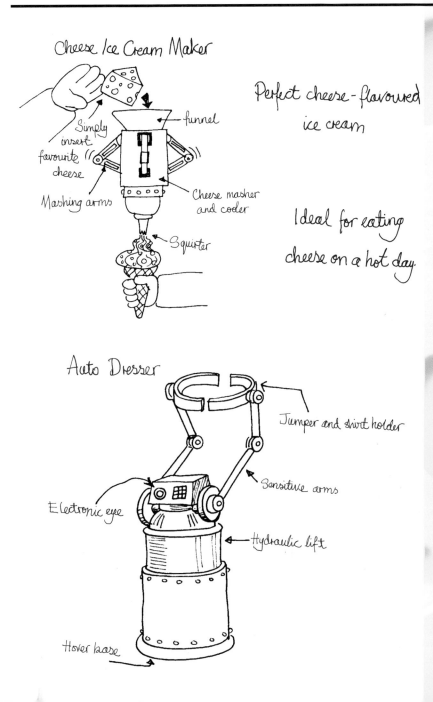

## Cheese Ice Cream Maker

Simply insert favourite cheese

Mashing arms

funnel

Cheese masher and cooler

Squirter

Perfect cheese-flavoured ice cream

Ideal for eating cheese on a hot day.

## Auto Dresser

Jumper and shirt holder

Sensitive arms

Electronic eye

Hydraulic lift

Hover base

# NOTES

## CHEESE BOARD

Dear Wallace

I'm writing to acknowledge receipt of your patent applications for a variety of ground-breaking cheese inventions.

Although we fully appreciate the amount of time and thought that must have been involved in these very original ideas (the 'Cheese Air Freshener' was a particular favourite), I have serious doubts of the marketability of these concepts. I also feel just a little concerned whether they would meet the Patent Health and Safety Standards – your Automatic Dairy Maker and the unsavoury Creamy Wallaby affair springs to mind.

As a fellow cheese-lover myself, I wouldn't want to discourage your innovative hobby in a way, but could I kindly ask you to refrain from sending in any more submissions for the time being. This is largely due to the lack of administrative staff to deal with the volume of inventions you send in and the unfortunate number of accidents that have resulted from testing some of your more 'ambitious' projects.

Yours regretfully.

*A. E. Butterworth*

(chairman)

He's obviously impressed, but I suppose I should hold off for a while.

Thank goodness.
G.

# CHEESE SOUVENIRS

The prize winners at Cheddar Gorge

YE OLDE CHEESE SHOPPE

The best store in town.

Must go back next year. G.

First published in 1997 by BBC Children's Publishing
a division of BBC Worldwide Ltd
Woodlands, 80 Wood Lane, London, W12 0TT
Text by Geoff Tibballs copyright © 1997 Wallace & Gromit Ltd
Illustrations by Stuart Trotter copyright © 1997 Wallace & Gromit Ltd
Design by Unlimited copyright © 1997 BBC Children's Publishing
Wallace & Gromit ™ and copyright © Wallace & Gromit Ltd, 1989
a member of the Aardman Animations group of companies.

ISBN 0 563 38047 0

Printed by Cambus Litho, East Kilbride